WOULD YOU RATHER

BOOK FOR KIDS

Christmas & Winter Edition

Fun, Hilarious, Ridiculous and
Challenging Questions for Kids,
Teens and the Whole Family

Jake Jokester

Check Out Other Fun Books
by Jake Jokester!

For every occasion

Camping Edition

Yuck! Edition

Gamer's Edition

Travel Edition

How to Play
~The Rules~

- You need at least 2 players to play.

- Choose who will go first. The first player chooses a question for the next player (player 2) to answer.

- Player 2 chooses one answer out of the 2 options.

You cannot answer "both" or "neither".

Optional rule: the answering player has to explain why they made the choice that they made.

- The player who answered the last question becomes the next asker. If there are more than 2 players, you can either pick any person to answer the next question or you can just ask the person next to you, going around in a circle.

Most important rule: Laugh, smile and have lots of fun!

★ ★ ★ ★ ★

Thanks for getting our book!

If you enjoy using it and it gives you lots of laughs
and fun moments, we would appreciate your review
on Amazon. Just head on over to this book's
Amazon page and click "Write a customer review."

We read each and every one of them.

★ ★ ★ ★ ★

Would You Rather...

sweat gravy

OR

sweat mashed potatoes?

give cash as a gift

OR

give a gift that you made for 10 hours?

Would You Rather...

have the courage
of a cow

OR

have the wisdom
of an owl?

eat a whole turkey

OR

drink gravy for a day?

Would You Rather...

get lost in the Alps

OR

find yourself amongst elves?

eat a candy cane sandwich

OR

eat candy corn pasta?

have everything you touch
turn to ice

OR

have everything you touch
turn to gold?

live in a house
with a fireplace

OR

live in a house with a pool?

be woken by
Christmas carols

OR

be woken by church bells?

have a storm
in a teacup

OR

be able to bottle joy?

run barefoot in the snow

OR

run barefoot on hot coal?

stay awake through
Christmas Eve

OR

stay awake through
New Year's Eve?

Would You Rather...

have a winter-less Christmas

OR

have sunny New Year's eve?

spend a year in an igloo

OR

spend a day next to
an active volcano?

Would You Rather...

rock around the
Christmas tree

OR

roll on a snowy hill?

eat ice cream on Christmas

OR

eat hot soup in the summer?

8

Would You Rather...

have holiday decorations
all year round

OR

never able to put up any holiday
decorations again?

play in the snow

OR

play in the windy cold?

Would You Rather...

eat stuffed turkey

OR

go without eating on Christmas but have a stocking stuffed with gifts?

have a snowball fight with friends

OR

build a snowman with friends?

Would You Rather...

sleep through the
coming of the first snow

OR

sleep through the coming
of the New Year?

shovel snow

OR

chop firewood?

Would You Rather...

Christmas lasted
all year long

OR

every day was
New Years?

fly a kite in
an ice storm

OR

drink iced tea in a
college dorm?

Would You Rather...

get many small presents
for Christmas

OR

get one big present
for Christmas?

exchange gifts
with strangers

OR

exchange postcards
with family?

Would You Rather...

skip Christmas dinner

OR

skip Christmas gifts?

pull Santa's sleigh

OR

lift pumpkins?

have mistletoe hanging in
your bedroom

OR

have mistletoe hanging in
your doorway?

travel on a cloud

OR

travel with Santa Claus?

Would You Rather...

go on a sleigh ride

OR

go on a horse ride?

only receive gifts on Christmas

OR

only give gifts on Christmas?

Would You Rather...

be visited by an angel
for Christmas

OR

be someone's Christmas miracle?

wear two pairs
of socks

OR

wear two pairs
of trousers?

Would You Rather...

make presents
for your family

OR

buy presents
for your family?

spend Christmas
at the beach

OR

spend Christmas
in your bed?

sit on Santa's lap

OR

make snow angels?

have to go to school during Christmas

OR

have the flu during your birthday?

Would You Rather...

always know the perfect gift
for someone else

OR

always receive the perfect
gift from others?

be out of wrapping paper

OR

be out of baking paper?

build a gingerbread house

OR

eat a gingerbread man?

go snowshoeing

OR

go snowboarding?

Would You Rather...

be someone's secret Santa

OR

be someone's secret admirer?

donate time
for the holidays

OR

donate money
for the holidays?

Would You Rather...

eat a whole turkey
by yourself

OR

never be able to eat
turkey again?

?

play with twenty puppies

OR

eat twenty hush puppies?

Would You Rather...

live inside a snow globe

OR

live in a fairytale?

get caught in
a snowstorm

OR

get caught in
a sandstorm?

Would You Rather...

have one extra gift

OR

one extra day off in school?

live in a ski lodge

OR

live in an igloo?

Would You Rather...

watch a hockey match

OR

watch a figure
skating competition?

have a carrot for a nose

OR

have a nose that glows
in the dark?

Would You Rather...

get a fun gift

OR

get a useful gift?

have someone do something
good for you but remain anonymous

OR

have someone do something good
and you know who they are?

Would You Rather...

eat icicles

OR

have popsicles fall
on your head?

not snow on
Christmas day

OR

it will snow all
year long?

Would You Rather...

be suddenly cold

OR

be suddenly old?

bury your legs
in the snow

OR

bury your head
in the sand?

Would You Rather...

find a box with
Christmas ornaments

OR

find a box with old letters?

spend the holidays
with your family

OR

spend the holidays with
your close friends?

Would You Rather...

watch the
New Year's Eve firework

OR

watch the 4th of July fireworks?

get stuck inside a chimney

OR

be stuck in your classroom?

Would You Rather...

hibernate all winter

OR

take a siesta all summer?

swap toys with friends

OR

swap clothes with
your siblings?

Would You Rather...

volunteer in a soup kitchen

OR

give your old toys
to goodwill?

ride a reindeer

OR

ride in Santa's sleigh?

Would You Rather...

sing Let it Snow

OR

sing Let it Go?

find hot coals in your Christmas stocking

OR

find hot coals in your bed?

eat Thanksgiving food
every day

OR

not eat Thanksgiving food
ever again?

wear a Santa hat

OR

wear a clown's nose?

Would You Rather...

enter the house through the chimney

OR

enter the house through the plumbing system?

get nothing for Christmas

OR

not eat candy for a whole year?

Would You Rather...

have snow every day
during holiday

OR

have no snow at all
for a whole year?

be allergic to cats

OR

be allergic to candy?

Would You Rather...

give away your favorite toy

OR

give away your
favorite clothes?

climb a snowy mountain

OR

walk on a frozen sea?

Would You Rather...

eat candy corn everyday

OR

eat candy cane everyday?

stay at home and have
lots of presents

OR

go somewhere nice and
enjoy the holiday?

Would You Rather...

make your own
holiday cards

OR

make your own
holiday cookies?

ride a snowmobile

OR

ride the batmobile?

visit all your relatives
for the holidays

OR

have all your relatives
visit you for the holidays?

light a Christmas tree

OR

light a candle?

Would You Rather...

make paper snowflakes

OR

make paper angels?

be a teddy bear

OR

be a polar bear?

Would You Rather...

be on Santa's nice list

OR

have sugar, spice and everything nice?

make an advent calendar

OR

go on a winter adventure?

Would You Rather...

have a fancy luxury holiday

OR

have a simple, homey holiday?

visit North Pole

OR

visit Bethlehem?

Would You Rather...

watch cartoons
on Christmas day

OR

go to the movies
on New Years Eve?

go Christmas caroling

OR

go trick-or-treating?

Would You Rather...

live in a huge
gingerbread house

OR

live in a huge dollhouse?

meet Ebenezer Scrooge

OR

meet Scrooge Mcduck?

Would You Rather...

eat a fruit mince pie

OR

eat a fruitcake?

invent a new holiday

OR

make a holiday fall
on your birthday?

Would You Rather...

travel during holidays

OR

stay at home?

be Rudolf
the red-nosed reindeer

OR

be Frosty the Snowman?

Would You Rather...

knit your own blanket

OR

sew your own
Christmas stockings?

be given new ski boots

OR

be given new skates?

Would You Rather...

go dog sledding

OR

go reindeer sledding?

have your home
smell likeww turkey

OR

have your home
smells like gravy?

Would You Rather...

make your own ornaments
for the tree

OR

not decorate
a tree at all?

travel during the holidays

OR

get to know your
town better?

Would You Rather...

sleep on a dog sled

OR

sleep in the doghouse?

lose your ski mask

OR

lose your Christmas stockings?

Would You Rather...

see an avalanche

OR

see an iceberg?

be snowed in at home

OR

be snowed in while
in a ski cabin?

Would You Rather...

eat roast turkey
for Christmas

OR

eat tofurkey (tofu-turkey)
for Christmas?

have cold toes

OR

take a cold shower?

Would You Rather...

go back and experience again
a great winter holiday

OR

get to travel to a
future winter holiday?

eat a candied apple

OR

eat a candy cane?

Would You Rather...

give presents to everyone
on Christmas

OR

give no presents, and declare your
presence as everyone's present
on Christmas Eve?

have pointy ears
like an elf

OR

have horns
like a reindeer?

Would You Rather...

go around the world
in 80 days

OR

go around the world
in one night?

decorate one real
Christmas tree

OR

decorate many
small plastic ones?

Would You Rather...

open your presents
a day late

OR

open one present
every day?

play with a toy train

OR

train your pet to
play with you?

Would You Rather...

wear a Santa costume
all day

OR

wear an elf costume
all day?

read a Christmas story

OR

write a Christmas story?

Would You Rather...

wear a reindeer sweater

OR

wear socks shaped like elves' shoes?

your grandma made you a quilt

OR

that she made you a sandwich?

Would You Rather...

have Santa's beard

OR

have Santa's belly?

ride a polar bear

OR

ride a cloud?

Would You Rather...

have your Christmas
wish come true

OR

keep your New Year's
resolution all year long?

wear a velvet bow
on your head

OR

wear a paper star
on your hat?

Would You Rather...

wrap a thousand presents

OR

bake a thousand cookies?

be Santa's reindeer Dasher

OR

be Santa's reindeer Dancer?

Would You Rather...

have Mrs. Claus for
your grandma

OR

have Santa Claus as
your teacher?

visit faraway family

OR

visit faraway friends?

Would You Rather...

meet the three wise men
from the East

OR

travel to the East yourself?

go ice skating

OR

go get ice cream?

Would You Rather...

the whole house smelled
like cinnamon

OR

your room smelled
like cheese?

write letters to Santa

OR

write emails to Santa?

Would You Rather...

cook for the holiday event

OR

clean up after the
holiday event?

wear fur boots

OR

have a fur coat?

Would You Rather...

be one of Santa's reindeers

OR

be one of Santa's elves?

eat frozen grapes

OR

drink melted ice cream?

Would You Rather...

ski on vanilla ice cream

OR

skate on strawberry jelly?

have winter holidays

OR

have summer holidays?

Would You Rather...

be on Santa's naughty list

OR

lose your mom's shopping list?

go on a polar expedition

OR

see a solar eclipse?

Would You Rather...

be visited by Grinch

OR

be visited by Krampus?

talk to a cartoon

OR

talk to the moon?

Would You Rather...

have December lasted
all year long

OR

that your birthday lasted
for a week?

take pictures of
holiday lights

OR

take pictures of
the Northern lights?

Would You Rather...

wear festive clothes
all year long

OR

wear your bathing suit
all year long?

slip on ice

OR

slip on a banana peel?

Would You Rather...

make cutout cookies

OR

have your work
cut out for you?

get stuck in an airport
during Christmas

OR

get stuck in an airport
on New Year's Eve?

Would You Rather...

work with Santa's elves

OR

study with Santa's reindeer?

spend summer in Antarctica

OR

spend winter in the desert?

have ribbons on
your shoes

OR

tie a shoelace to
your hair?

sleep watching the fireplace

OR

sleep listening to the rain?

Would You Rather...

open other people's gifts

OR

have your gifts opened by others?

swim in shaved ice

OR

swim in powdered sugar?

Would You Rather...

be visited by the ghosts
of Christmas past

OR

visit the ghosts
of Hogwarts?

watch dancing on ice

OR

watch dancing mice?

78

Would You Rather...

hear hooves on the roof

OR

hear a thud in
the living room?

wear earmuffs

OR

eat muffins?

Would You Rather...

plant a Christmas tree

OR

plant an avocado tree?

be Santa Claus

OR

Rudolf the red-nosed reindeer?

Would You Rather...

have presents under the tree

OR

have presents under your bed?

---

see the star of Bethlehem

OR

see a shooting star?

Would You Rather...

ring the bell of
a haunted house

OR

sing Jingle Bells
all night long?

meet a snow fox

OR

meet a snow leopard?

Would You Rather...

be born in a manger

OR

be born in a mansion?

eat cranberry sauce

OR

have blueberry pie?

Would You Rather...

have a long garland

OR

have a long tail?

go to school on
a cable car

OR

go home on a dog sled?

Would You Rather...

make a sculpture
out of ice

OR

make a sculpture
out of chocolate?

hang string lights
from the ceiling

OR

hang mistletoe
above the door?

sneeze over mistletoe

OR

stub your toe?

build a gingerbread skyscraper

OR

drink a sip of butter beer?

Would You Rather...

go to the North Pole and
remove any flags planted there

OR

go to the South Pole and
plant your flag there?

go ice skating on a lake

OR

go skiing on a mountain?

Would You Rather...

have 12 reindeers

OR

8 days of Christmas?

drink warm milk
before bed

OR

drink hot cocoa
before bed?

Would You Rather...

wear red and green

OR

wear white,
red and black?

be a kid during holidays

OR

be a grandparent
during holidays?

Would You Rather...

have a coloring book

OR

have a cookbook?

count down to
the New Year

OR

count down to a
space shuttle launch?

Would You Rather...

play cards with
your parents

OR

play fetch with
your pet?

have a partridge in
a pear tree

OR

an angel on a
Christmas tree?

Would You Rather...

eat a thousand raisins

OR

eat a thousand peanuts?

play snowball fights

OR

watch snow fall?

Would You Rather...

go shopping for gifts

OR

go shopping for candy?

receive a letter
from Santa

OR

receive a letter
from Hogwarts?

Would You Rather...

have Christmas tree tinsel
as your hair

OR

have Christmas lights in
your fingernails?

meet Father Christmas

OR

meet Mother Teresa?

Would You Rather...

live in a winter wonderland

OR

visit Alice in Wonderland?

play the triangle

OR

play the harmonica?

Would You Rather...

visit Santa's toy factory

OR

visit Willy Wonka's chocolate factory?

leave milk and cookies for Santa

OR

leave a tooth for the tooth fairy?

Would You Rather...

have a red-nose
like Rudolph

OR

have a red coat
like Santa?

run in the snow

OR

roll in the snow?

Would You Rather...

have frosty feet

OR

have no frosting
on your cake?

spill your hot cocoa

OR

spill the eggnog?

Would You Rather...

have your own ice rink

OR

have a diamond ring?

meet Frosty the Snowman

OR

meet Blixen the reindeer?

Would You Rather...

have a cold during the holidays

OR

have cold weather all year long?

wrap presents

OR

shop for presents?

One last thing - we would love to hear
your feedback about this book!

If you found this activity book fun and useful, we
would be very grateful if you posted a short review on
Amazon! Your support does make a difference and we
read every review personally.

If you would like to leave a review, just head on
over to this book's Amazon page and click
"Write a customer review."

Thank you for your support!

★ ★ ★ ★ ★

Check Out Other Fun Books
by Jake Jokester!

For every occasion

Yuck! Edition

Camping Edition

Gamer's Edition

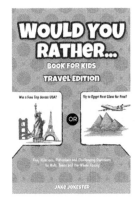

Travel Edition

Made in United States
North Haven, CT
26 November 2021

11545976R00063